TOP BRANDS

TIKTOK

BY BECKY NOELLE

WWW.APEXEDITIONS.COM

Copyright © 2024 by Apex Editions, Mendota Heights, MN 55120. All rights reserved. No part of this book may be reproduced or utilized in any form or by any means without written permission from the publisher.

Apex is distributed by North Star Editions:
sales@northstareditions.com | 888-417-0195

Produced for Apex by Red Line Editorial.

Photographs ©: Shutterstock Images, cover, 1, 8–9, 13, 14, 16–17, 20, 22–23, 24, 25, 26, 27, 29; iStockphoto, 4–5, 6, 21; Stringer/Imaginechina/AP Images, 10–11; Christian Charisius/dpa picture alliance/Alamy, 12; Leco Viana/TheNEWS2/ZUMA Press, Inc./Alamy, 15; Drew Angerer/Getty Images News/Getty Images, 18–19

Library of Congress Control Number: 2022920697

ISBN
978-1-63738-569-2 (hardcover)
978-1-63738-623-1 (paperback)
978-1-63738-726-9 (ebook pdf)
978-1-63738-677-4 (hosted ebook)

Printed in the United States of America
Mankato, MN
082023

NOTE TO PARENTS AND EDUCATORS

Apex books are designed to build literacy skills in striving readers. Exciting, high-interest content attracts and holds readers' attention. The text is carefully leveled to allow students to achieve success quickly. Additional features, such as bolded glossary words for difficult terms, help build comprehension.

TABLE OF CONTENTS

CHAPTER 1
USING TIKTOK 4

CHAPTER 2
TIKTOK HISTORY 10

CHAPTER 3
TIKTOK TODAY 16

CHAPTER 4
TIKTOK FAMOUS 22

COMPREHENSION QUESTIONS • 28
GLOSSARY • 30
TO LEARN MORE • 31
ABOUT THE AUTHOR • 31
INDEX • 32

CHAPTER 1

A girl is done with her homework. She's ready to relax. She opens TikTok. A dance video plays. It's her favorite TikToker!

Homework can be stressful. A fun app such as TikTok is one way to relax.

The girl laughs. She sends the video to her friend. Her friend asks to come over. They watch the dance again. Then they practice copying it.

POPULAR VIDEOS

Most people enjoy TikTok videos that are musical or funny. Videos about beauty are also popular. Tricks and surprise endings often get lots of views, too.

◀ Many people learn new dance moves by watching videos.

Some TikTok dances spread all around the world. People in many countries learn and share them.

Once the friends are ready, they open TikTok. They perform and record the dance. The girl tags her friend. She posts it to her account.

FAST FACT

TikTok became the most popular app in 2020. It was downloaded 850 million times.

CHAPTER 2

TIKTOK HISTORY

TikTok was started in China by ByteDance. The company studied 100 other video apps to make TikTok. ByteDance wanted TikTok to be easy and fun.

Zhang Yiming started ByteDance in 2012.

Lisa and Lena Mantler were some of the first stars on Musical.ly. The German twins have millions of followers on TikTok.

By 2017, people throughout Asia could get TikTok. Then ByteDance added Musical.ly to TikTok in 2018. Musical.ly was a **lip-synching** app.

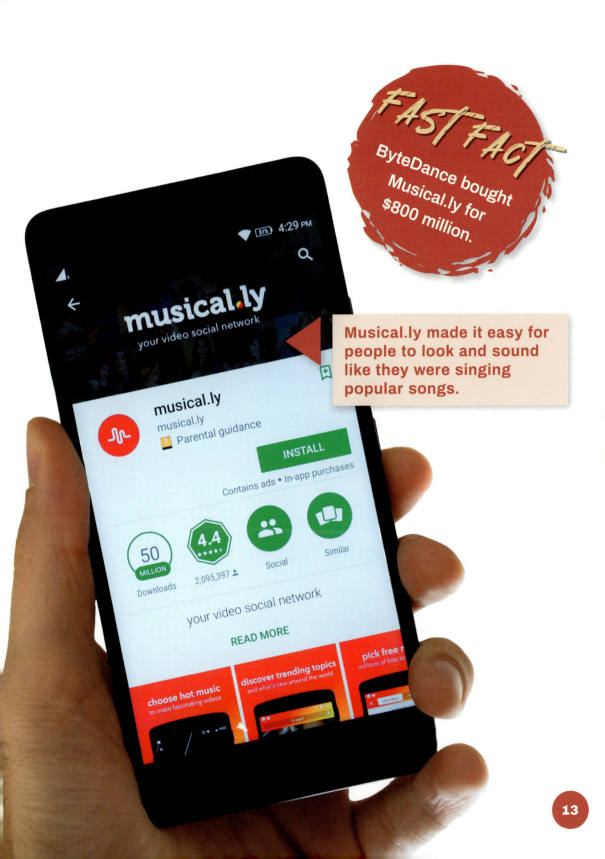

FAST FACT
ByteDance bought Musical.ly for $800 million.

Musical.ly made it easy for people to look and sound like they were singing popular songs.

TikTok's watermark includes a mostly white version of its logo, which is usually black. It shows up when videos are played on other apps.

Teenagers were the first TikTok users. They shared videos on other **social media**. Other people saw the TikTok **watermark**. They started using TikTok, too. TikTok spread around the world.

TOP COUNTRIES

In 2022, the United States was home to the most TikTok users. It had more than 130 million. Indonesia had nearly 100 million users. Brazil had almost 75 million.

Pietra Amaral is from São Paolo, Brazil. She became a TikTok star as a teenager.

CHAPTER 3

TIKTOK TODAY

TikTok is known for its short, funny videos. TikTokers record their videos in the app. They can add sounds, **effects**, and filters.

Some people use stands and other tools to help record TikTok videos.

TikTokers can use effects from other videos. For example, they can copy speech. Those words can be funny or strange in a new video.

Fast Fact

In 2021, 25 percent of US TikTok users were between 10 and 19 years old.

◀ TikTokers often have to make videos every day to become popular.

19

The top TikTok videos can get more than one billion views.

Users can like videos or add comments. They can share videos with friends or save them for later.

STAYING SAFE

TikTok uses endless scroll. New videos appear as the user moves down the screen. As a result, it can be hard to stop watching. However, too much screen time is not healthy.

Too much screen time can cause problems with people's eyes, sleep, and more.

21

CHAPTER 4

TIKTOK FAMOUS

Many TikTokers make videos that are just for fun. But some teach people new skills. Others **recommend** books.

Videos go viral when lots of people watch and like the video.

Charli D'Amelio made millions of dollars on TikTok in 2022.

Some people get famous on TikTok. Companies pay them to help sell products. Top TikTokers can earn more than $250,000 for a sponsored video.

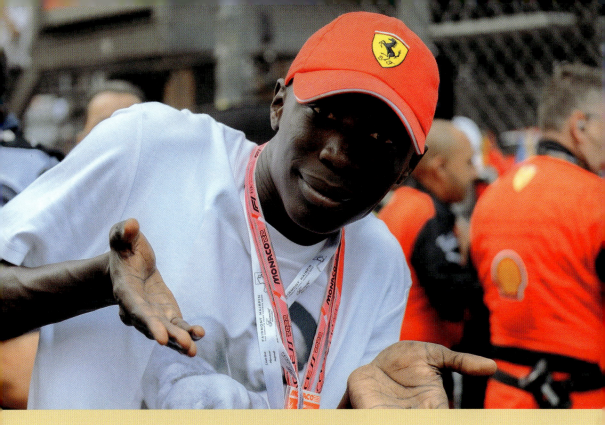

Khaby Lame became known for his funny TikToks. He often made faces as he looked right at the camera.

FAST FACT

In 2022, Khaby Lame was the top TikToker. He had more than 153 million followers.

In 2022, TikTok was worth billions of dollars.

TikTok uses an **algorithm**. This program gathers user's **data**. For example, it tracks the videos a user does and doesn't like. Then it suggests new ones. These videos are **specific** to each user.

DATA WORRIES

User data helps companies **advertise**. But many people worry how their data is used. It could be used to track their location. Or the data could be used to shape their actions.

TikTokers can use Creator Marketplace to advertise products. ByteDance made Creator Marketplace in 2020.

COMPREHENSION QUESTIONS

Write your answers on a separate piece of paper.

1. Write a paragraph summarizing what users can do on TikTok.

2. Would you want to be TikTok famous? Why or why not?

3. Which company started TikTok?
    - A. Musical.ly
    - B. Creator Marketplace
    - C. ByteDance

4. Why is user data helpful for TikTok's algorithm?
    - A. It helps TikTok stop videos from spreading.
    - B. It helps TikTok find unsafe videos.
    - C. It helps TikTok get better at showing videos that users like.

5. What does **scroll** mean in this book?

*TikTok uses endless **scroll**. New videos appear as the user moves down the screen.*

    A. moving up or down
    B. starting over
    C. using paper

6. What does **sponsored** mean in this book?

*Companies pay them to help sell products. Top TikTokers can earn as much as $250,000 for a **sponsored** video.*

    A. deleted from the internet
    B. made for free
    C. used to help sell something

Answer key on page 32.

GLOSSARY

advertise
To try to get people to buy something.

algorithm
Steps that a computer follows to finish a process.

data
Information collected to study or track something.

effects
Ways to add details and change how videos look.

lip-synching
Pretending to sing by moving one's lips.

recommend
To suggest something a person might like.

social media
Apps or websites that let people connect online.

specific
Having to do with a certain person or thing.

watermark
A permanent mark on something to show where it came from.

BOOKS

Coombes, Sharie. *Online Offline!: An Activity Book for Young People Who Want to Lead a Healthy Digital Life*. London: Bonnier Books, 2021.

Miller, Marie-Therese. *Social Media Addiction*. San Diego: Reference Point Press, 2023.

Scholastic. *The Ultimate Guide to TikTok*. New York: Scholastic, 2020.

ONLINE RESOURCES

Visit **www.apexeditions.com** to find links and resources related to this title.

ABOUT THE AUTHOR

Becky Noelle edits and writes children's nonfiction books. This is the 16th book she has written. Becky loves writing because she always gets to learn new things. She learned a lot of fascinating things about TikTok writing this book!

INDEX

A
algorithm, 26
apps, 9, 10, 12, 16

B
Brazil, 15
ByteDance, 10, 12–13

C
China, 10
companies, 10, 24, 27

D
dance videos, 4, 7–8
data, 26–27

E
endless scroll, 21

I
Indonesia, 15

L
Lame, Khaby, 25

M
Musical.ly, 12–13

S
social media, 14
sponsored videos, 24

T
TikTokers, 4, 16, 19, 22, 24–25

U
United States, 15, 19

ANSWER KEY:
1. Answers will vary; 2. Answers will vary; 3. C; 4. C; 5. A; 6. C